ICE FISHING

BY KARA L. LAUGHLIN

Published by The Child's World®
1980 Lookout Drive • Mankato, MN 56003-1705
800-599-READ • www.childsworld.com

ACKNOWLEDGMENTS
The Child's World®: Mary Swensen, Publishing Director
The Design Lab: Design
Heidi Hogg: Editing
Sarah M. Miller: Editing

PHOTO CREDITS
© Alexander Lukatskiy/Shutterstock.com: 2-3, 10; Andrey
Oleshko/Shutterstock.com: 13; dcwcreations/Shutterstock.com:
cover, 1; Johanna Phillips Huuva/Shutterstock.com: 4; Maksym
Sukhenko/Shutterstock.com: 15; Martins Vanags/Shutterstock.
com: 20-21; Natalia D/Shutterstock.com: 9; Natalia Gaak
NWH/Shutterstock.com: 19; PEPPERSMINT/Shutterstock.com: 7;
V. J. Matthew/Shutterstock.com: 16-17

ISBN: 9781503807785
LCCN: 2015958114

Printed in the United States of America
Mankato, MN
June, 2016
PA02300

TABLE OF CONTENTS

4

Winter Fishing

In the winter, ice covers the lakes of northern areas. All the fish move to the bottom of the lakes. To catch those fish, you must go ice fishing.

Fast Fact!
Snow often covers the ice on frozen lakes.

Safe Ice

The first thing ice fishers do is check the ice. It must be thick enough to walk on. People use an ice **chisel** to chip through the ice. They chip until they hit the water.

They measure the ice. It must be at least 4 inches (10 centimeters) thick to walk on.

Fast Fact!

When ice is thicker than 12 inches (30 cm), even pickup trucks can drive on it!

Augers

At the fishing site, it is time to cut a hole. Ice fishers use an **auger** to make a hole in the ice. The auger looks like a giant drill. You turn the handle to make it cut into the ice. It makes a hole just big enough for a fish to go through.

Fast Fact!
The world's largest ice fishing contest is held every year in Minnesota.

Ice Skimmers

Slush will form around the hole. An ice **skimmer** clears it away. A skimmer looks like a flat spoon with holes. The water drains through the holes. Then you can lift up the slush.

Fast Fact!
Canada has the most ice fishers.

Drop the Line

Time to drop the **line**! First, put on your **bait**. Next, drop the line through the hole.

Some people use a **jiggle stick**. A jiggle stick is a short fishing rod. When you get a bite, you pull the line up by hand.

Fast Fact!
Worms, grubs, and minnows are great bait for ice fishing.

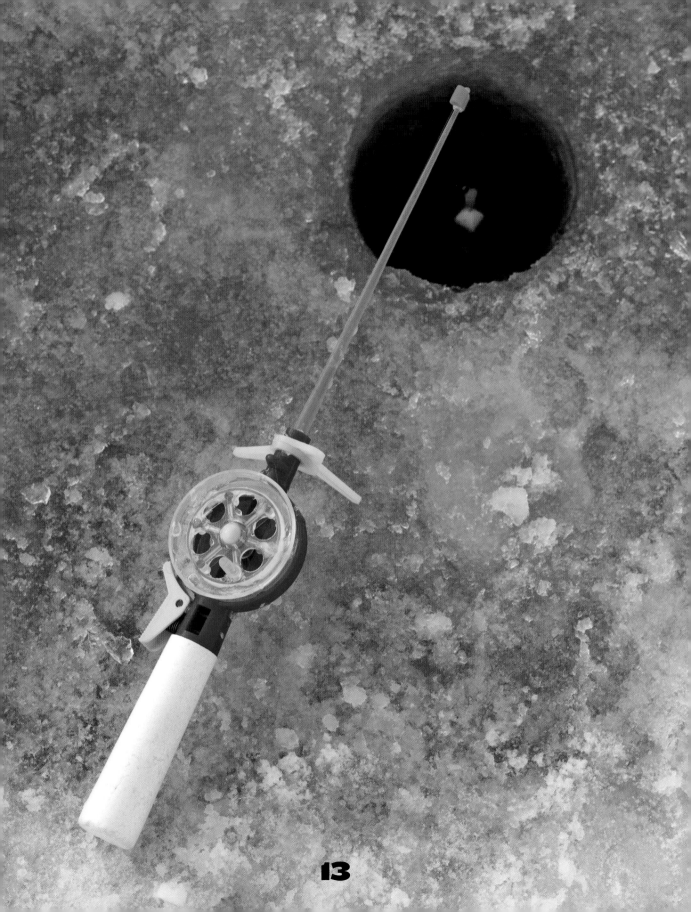

13

Tip-Ups

Did a fish just bite? It is hard to know. A **tip-up** shows when a fish takes the bait. When the fish pulls the bait, a flag pops up.

Fast Fact!
Tip-ups got their name because the flag "tips up" when a fish is on.

Ice Shanties

You may wait a long time before a fish bites. You need to keep warm while you wait.

An **ice shanty** is a tent or building on the lake. You can go in the shanty to take a break and warm up. Some have beds and stoves inside!

Fish On!

Up pops the flag! Time to pull in the line. Pull slowly—you do not want to break the line. Soon, you will see the fish. When you do, pull it up through the hole.

18

As the days get warmer, the ice gets weak. It is time to take the shanty off the lake. No more ice fishing until next year!

Fast Fact!

Less than half of all fish caught through ice fishing are eaten. Most are released back into the lake.

Glossary

auger (AW-ger): A tool used to drill a hole into the ice. The user twists the handle to drive the sharp edges into the ice.

bait (BAYT): A small amount of food used to lure a fish into putting its mouth around a hook. Ice fishers often use a worm or a small fish as bait.

chisel (CHIZ-ul): A hand tool used for chopping into the ice. A chisel is a long pole that ends with a metal edge.

ice shanty (ICE SHAN-tee): A temporary shelter for people to use while out on the ice is called an ice shanty.

jiggle stick (JIG-gul STIK): A jiggle stick is a type of short fishing rod without a reel, often used in ice fishing.

line (LINE): The nylon string that attaches the bait to the fishing pole is called a line.

skimmer (SKIM-mur): A tool for taking slush out of an ice-fishing hole. It looks like a ladle or plate with holes in it.

tip-up (TIP UP): A fishing tool that is attached to a fishing line. When a fish pulls the line, a flag on the tip-up pops up.

To Learn More

In the Library

Green, Sara. *Ice Fishing*. Minneapolis, MN: Bellwether Media, 2014.

Larson, Deborah Jo. *One Frozen Lake*. St. Paul, MN: Minnesota Historical Society Press, 2012.

Schwartz, Tina P. *Ice Fishing*. New York, NY: PowerKids Press, 2012.

On the Web

Visit our Web site for links about ice fishing: **childsworld.com/links**

Note to Parents, Teachers, and Librarians: We routinely verify our Web links to make sure they are safe and active sites. So encourage your readers to check them out!

Index

About the Author

Kara L. Laughlin is an artist and writer who lives in Virginia with her husband, three kids, two guinea pigs, and a dog. She is the author of two dozen nonfiction books for kids.